EVEREST
REACHING THE
WORLD'S
HIGHEST PEAK

In 1933, two aircraft set off to
make an aerial survey of Everest.

John Hunt gathered his team to
announce which climbers would
try for the summit.

The Sherpas who climbed to the highest camps in
the 1953 ascent of Everest. The toughest were
given the honorary title of "Tiger".

Just below the summit, Edmund Hillary
had to make his way up a narrow gap
between the rock and the ice.

Inside the tent, the two
men had a cold and
sleepless night.

Hillary and Tenzing struggled to put
up their tent on the South Ridge.

EVEREST
REACHING THE WORLD'S HIGHEST PEAK

Written by
RICHARD PLATT

Illustrated by
RUSSELL BARNET
and JOHN JAMES

Dorling Kindersley

Dorling **Kindersley**

LONDON, NEW YORK, SYDNEY, DELHI, PARIS,
MUNICH, AND JOHANNESBURG .

Project Editor Francesca Baines
Art Editor Sarah Ponder
Senior Editor Scarlett O'Hara
Deputy Managing Art Editor Vicky Wharton
Managing Editor Sue Grabham
Senior Managing Art Editor Julia Harris
DTP Designer Andrew O'Brien
Picture Researcher Pernilla Pearce
Jacket Designer Dean Price
Production Kate Oliver and Chris Avgherinos
Consultant Andy McNae, British
Mountaineering Council

First published in 2000
by Dorling Kindersley Limited,
9 Henrietta Street, Covent Garden,
London WC2E 8PS

2 4 6 8 10 9 7 5 3 1

A CIP catalogue record for this book is available
from the British Library.

ISBN 0 7513 6656 0

Reproduced by Colourscan, Singapore
Printed and bound by L.E.G.O., Italy

Additional illustrations by David Ashby,
Ann Winterbotham, and Sallie Alane Reason

see our complete catalogue at
www.dk.com

Contents

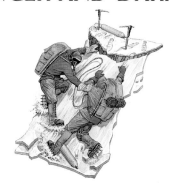

Paths to the top

MOUNTAINS HAVE ALWAYS PROVED A CHALLENGE TO THE PEOPLE who live in their shadow. Travel in mountainous areas is slow and difficult, and life on the slopes is harsh. But two hundred years ago, people began to see mountains as a new challenge. They wanted to climb as high as possible, and the greatest prize was the highest summit of all – Everest.

Snow on the high peaks melts to form icy streams, which flow into mountain lakes.

of the
World

An Alpine Lake painted
by Karl Millner
(1825–94)

THE FIRST MOUNTAIN EXPLORERS

UNTIL THE 18TH CENTURY, THERE WERE FEW visitors to the mountainous areas of the world. Then, the summits began to attract a new type of climber – scientists who studied the natural world and were attracted to the glaciers (rivers of ice) of Europe's Alps. They studied the rocks nearby, the climate, and the plants that grew on the lower slopes. They marvelled at the spectacular views and enjoyed the solitude. However, the scientists didn't have the mountains to themselves for long. By the end of the 18th century, people were climbing for the sheer thrill of it, and the dictionary had a new word: mountaineering – the sport of mountain climbing.

EXPLORING GLACIER

In the 18th century, scientists were both fascinated and terrified by the magnificent glaciers of the Alps. These rivers of ice creaked and cracked as they slowly advanced down the mountainside Only the most daring scientists actually climbed onto the ice.

LADDER MAN
For the steeper parts, climbers of Mont Blanc carried ladders.

The Iceman

THE EARLIEST KNOWN ALPINE explorer was an ancient traveller we now call Ötzi the Iceman. His body appeared in 1991 when the glacier that had preserved it for 5,300 years melted.

Ötzi's teeth reveal that he died in his late twenties.

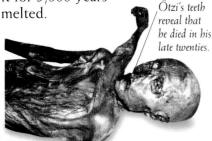

Personal possessions
Near the Iceman's body lay the equipment of an ancient traveller: a backpack, a fur cloak, food, a bow and arrows, a flint knife, and a copper axe. He may have been a shaman (priest), a hunter, or a trader.

Axe with copper head

Leather quiver

CLIMBING PARTY
A crowd of guides and porters accompanied Saussure on his ascent of Mont Blanc.

THE CHALLENGE OF MONT BLANC

Mountaineering as a sport began in 1760 when Swiss physicist Horace Bénédict de Saussure (1740–99) offered a prize to the first person to climb Mont Blanc. The peak lies on the French-Italian border, and at 4,807 m (15,770 ft) is Europe's highest. Saussure did not have to pay out the prize until 1786, when a doctor from Chamonix, the town at the foot of the mountain, reached the summit. The following year, Saussure himself climbed to the top of Mont Blanc.

FIRST VICTORY...

By the 19th century, Western Europe's greatest unclimbed mountain was the 4,478-m (14,692-ft) high Matterhorn, on the Swiss-Italian border. English artist Edward Whymper (1840–1911) was determined to be the first to the summit. He succeeded on his eighth attempt, in 1865, climbing to the top with three companions, two guides, and a porter.

The climbers made a flag from a shirt.

...THEN TRAGEDY

Whymper and his companions were delighted with their achievement. However, disaster struck as they descended. Climbing over smooth rocks, one of the group slipped and fell. The safety rope linking them all snapped, and four of the party fell to their deaths. The tragic accident ended Whymper's climbing career.

ANCHOR MEN
Whymper and the men tied to the top of the rope tried to stop the fall.

THIN ROPE
The safety rope was the thinnest of the three they were carrying.

NOVICE SLIPS
Douglas Hadow (1846–65), whose slip caused the accident, had little climbing experience.

DEADLY FALL
The four men tumbled down the mountain onto the glacier far below.

A POPULAR SPORT

The next group of people to discover the mountains were wealthy enthusiasts who, from the 1850s onwards, formed climbing clubs. Ten years later, travel agents Thomas Cook offered guided tours in the Alps. Climbing became really popular, however, when new railway lines brought less wealthy people to the peaks. The snooty pioneers complained about the crowds.

The Duke of Abruzzi
Many people consider the Duke of Abruzzi (1873–1933) the greatest mountaineering explorer of all time. The son of a Spanish king, he led many daring expeditions in the late 19th and early 20th centuries. He climbed in the Alps, Alaska, Africa, and the Himalayas. In 1909, he set a new record by climbing to 7,500 m (24,500 ft) on K2, now in Pakistan.

Himalayan pioneer
By the end of the 19th century, European climbers were looking beyond the Alps for excitement. Englishman, W.W. Graham (above) was among the first to climb in the Himalayas. In 1883, he and two Swiss guides scaled several peaks "purely for sport and adventure".

THE EARLY DAYS OF CLIMBING

IN THE 19TH CENTURY, MOUNTAINEERING became a serious sport, and climbers began to develop techniques to overcome the problems they encountered. Most climbers agree that mountaineering involves three main skills and these have not changed over time. Hiking is the first, and the easiest to learn. The second skill is rock climbing, because most mountains have some steep, bare rock. Finally, the highest peaks are frozen, even in summer, so climbers need to use snow- and ice-climbing techniques to reach the top.

Climbers were roped to their guide for safety.

Professional guides
Climbers in the 19th century relied on local guides to take them up a mountain. Englishman Edward Whymper owed his conquest of the Matterhorn in 1865 to the skills of Swiss guide Michel Croz (above).

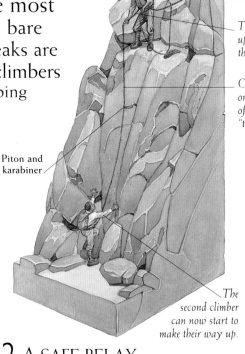

The rope is secured to the rock.

The leader takes up the slack in the rope.

Climbers call one rope-length of a climb "the pitch".

Piton and karabiner

The second climber can now start to make their way up.

To reduce the distance of a fall, the climber hammers in a piton (see box below) and passes the safety rope through it.

The climber at the bottom feeds out the rope.

1 CLIMBING ROCK
The leader begins to climb, tied to a safety rope. If the leader slips, the partner grips the rope. The leader will only fall the length of the rope between them and their partner.

2 A SAFE BELAY
At a safe point, the leader stops and ties the rope to the rock. They then "belay" their partner. This means that they prepare to stop them falling by holding on to the loose rope as the partner climbs.

3 AT THE TOP
Once the partner has reached the top, they climb the next pitch in the same way. If both climbers are equally skilled, they may take turns at the more dangerous job of leading.

Extra protection

UNTIL RECENTLY, climbers hammered steel spikes, called pitons, into the rock for extra safety. A rope was secured to the piton using a metal ring called a karabiner. Today, nuts and bolts (see page 39) have replaced pitons.

Safety ring
Karabiners open and shut so that ropes can slip on and off easily.

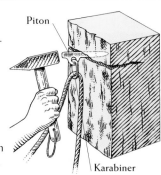

Piton

Karabiner

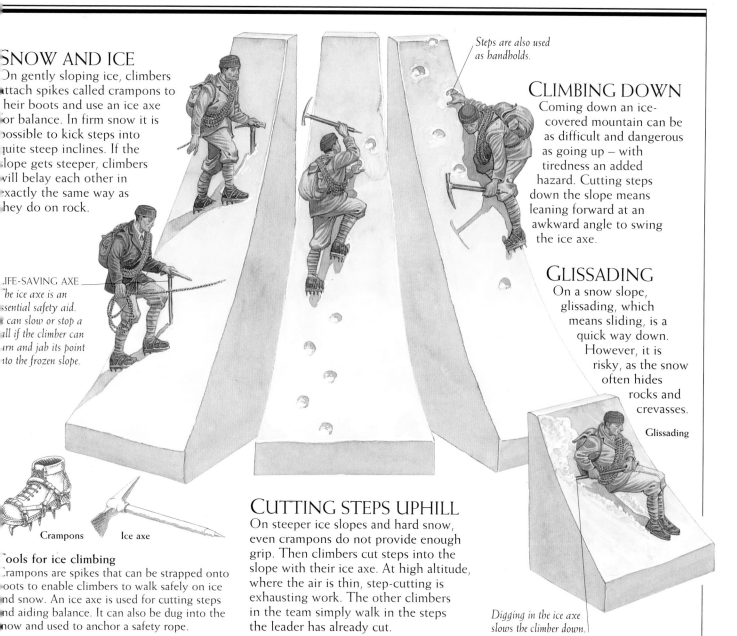

SNOW AND ICE

On gently sloping ice, climbers attach spikes called crampons to their boots and use an ice axe for balance. In firm snow it is possible to kick steps into quite steep inclines. If the slope gets steeper, climbers will belay each other in exactly the same way as they do on rock.

LIFE-SAVING AXE
The ice axe is an essential safety aid. It can slow or stop a fall if the climber can turn and jab its point into the frozen slope.

Crampons   Ice axe

Tools for ice climbing
Crampons are spikes that can be strapped onto boots to enable climbers to walk safely on ice and snow. An ice axe is used for cutting steps and aiding balance. It can also be dug into the snow and used to anchor a safety rope.

Steps are also used as handholds.

CLIMBING DOWN

Coming down an ice-covered mountain can be as difficult and dangerous as going up – with tiredness an added hazard. Cutting steps down the slope means leaning forward at an awkward angle to swing the ice axe.

GLISSADING

On a snow slope, glissading, which means sliding, is a quick way down. However, it is risky, as the snow often hides rocks and crevasses.

Glissading

CUTTING STEPS UPHILL

On steeper ice slopes and hard snow, even crampons do not provide enough grip. Then climbers cut steps into the slope with their ice axe. At high altitude, where the air is thin, step-cutting is exhausting work. The other climbers in the team simply walk in the steps the leader has already cut.

Digging in the ice axe slows the climber down.

Crossing a crevasse

WHEN WALKING on glaciers there is the added danger of crevasses. These cracks in the ice can be very deep, and snow often hides them. The leading climber of a roped team looks for the telltale signs. These are a slight hollow, or a dull tint to the snow. Crossing a crevasse requires great care.

1 A climber must either walk around a crevasse or cross on a snow bridge. The leading climber tests the bridge carefully with an ice axe before risking a crossing.

2 A good belay is essential to protect the leader in case the bridge collapses. The second climber secures the belay to an ice axe or to solid snow or ice.

3 Although the leader has crossed in safety, this does not prove that the snow bridge is secure. The leader must protect those who follow with a belay.

GASPING FOR BREATH

STARVED OF OXYGEN, FROZEN BY icy winds, and dazzled by brilliant sunshine, climbers on Everest face frightening difficulties. Other mountains demand more skill and strength, but Everest's height and climate make it specially dangerous. Thin air is the biggest hazard. At sea level, the air contains plenty of the oxygen we need for life, but as climbers go higher, levels of oxygen sink lower. Climbers gasp for breath and become weak and ill. At the top of Everest the air is so thin that it is impossible to survive for long.

> "We all began to feel sick from nausea and giddiness, which was far more distressing than our difficulties in breathing. Blood exuded from the lips and gums, and the eyes became bloodshot."
>
> The first description of mountain sickness, by German explorer Alexander von Humboldt (1769-1859), from *Personal Narrative of Travels to Equinoctial Regions of America*, 1852

EARLY EXPERIMENTS
In 1922, George Finch confirmed the value of extra oxygen on Everest

Running out of air

BREATHLESSNESS AND A FAST PULSE are the first signs of altitude sickness. Most people adapt to thin air (air low in oxygen) after a few days at moderate altitudes. Higher up, the only way to avoid more serious symptoms is to breathe oxygen from cylinders.

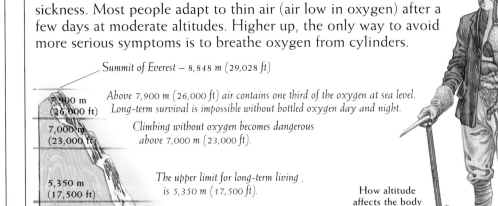

Summit of Everest – 8,848 m (29,028 ft)

7,900 m (26,000 ft) — Above 7,900 m (26,000 ft) air contains one third of the oxygen at sea level. Long-term survival is impossible without bottled oxygen day and night.

7,000 m (23,000 ft) — Climbing without oxygen becomes dangerous above 7,000 m (23,000 ft).

5,350 m (17,500 ft) — The upper limit for long-term living is 5,350 m (17,500 ft).

3,050, m 10,000 ft — At around 3,050 m (10,000 ft) people become breathless; some get headaches, but most adapt in two or three days.

Ample oxygen for comfortable breathing and vigorous exercise.

Sea level

Levels of oxygen at different altitudes

How altitude affects the body

Dizziness, poor concentration, headaches, muddled thinking and sleeplessness, leading eventually to unconsciousness.

Blurred vision and bloodshot eyes

Sore throat

Lungs become painful, and blood is coughed up. Fluid fills lungs.

Heart beats faster

Loss of appetite and vomiting

Limbs are very weak, cramp is common. Even minor effort causes exhaustion.

Effects of altitude
Everyone reacts differently to thin air, but on Everest all climbers suffer some of the symptoms above. The effects on the brain are perhaps the most dangerous, because sufferers may not even realise they are ill.

Numbness is the first sign of frostbite. Rubbing numb feet helps to keep the blood circulating and can prevent frostbite.

FROSTBITE

The cold winds of Everest quickly freeze flesh. The result is frostbite – the affected area goes numb and grey. If frostbite is severe, flesh can die and rot. Extra-warm clothes and boots help prevent this, but many Everest climbers have lost toes, which freeze first.

Snow-blindness
Sunlit snow can cause temporary blindness in climbers who do not protect their eyes. When supplies ran out, the British 1953 expedition made these makeshift sunglasses from cardboard and tinted plastic for their Sherpa guides and porters on Everest.

Sherpas called the bottled oxygen "English air".

The rucksack frame supported the steel cylinders.

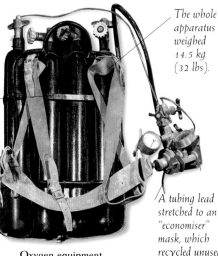

The whole apparatus weighed 14.5 kg (32 lbs).

A tubing lead stretched to an "economiser" mask, which recycled unused oxygen to save on gas.

Oxygen equipment from 1922

EXTRA OXYGEN

As early as 1907 climbers tried fighting mountain sickness by breathing oxygen from cylinders. Serious use of the gas began only in the 1920s, after British climbers George Finch and Geoffrey Bruce tested it on Everest. They proved that use of oxygen enabled them to survive at high altitude. It also improved stamina, even though cylinders were heavy. However, some climbers considered that using oxygen was unsporting.

eoffrey Bruce lped Finch test e oxygen sets at 400 m (21,000 ft).

FACT file

- Going down the mountain as little as 100 m (330 ft) is often enough to cure mild altitude sickness.
- Climbers rarely die of altitude sickness, but because it impairs judgement, fatal accidents are more likely.
- Around 90% of frostbite occurs in fingers and toes.
- Snow-blindness causes great pain but rarely lasts longer than a few days.

Sickness relief

TODAY, PEOPLE SUFFERING from altitude sickness can get relief in a hyperbaric chamber or Gamow® bag. Pumping air into the sealed bag produces the same effect as descending the mountain.

Air-tight zip

A safety valve stops pressure rising too high.

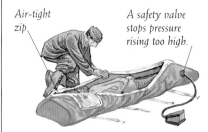

Getting in
The chamber can treat climbers who are too ill to descend. Fit comrades help the sick climber into the deflated bag, and zip up the opening.

Plastic window

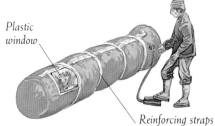

Reinforcing straps

Pumping up
A foot pump inflates the chamber, forcing extra oxygen into the lungs of the patient. Pumping, which takes about an hour, is hard work.

Towards Everest

IN NEPAL THE MOUNTAIN'S NAME is Sagarmatha; to Tibetans it is Chomolunga. Both names mean the same: "Goddess mother of the world". The surveyors who measured the mountain in 1852 had less imagination. They called it "Peak XV". When expeditions to climb it began in 1920, the mountain was already known by the name we use today: Everest.

The Buddhists of Tibet believe that Everest and other Himalayan mountains are the homes of the gods.

High peaks ring a mythical paradise called Shambala, with palaces and gardens at its centre.

A Buddhist painting called a mandala, which represents the universe.

Map of the world showing the area covered in the more detailed map below

The Himalayas lie along the border of China with India, Nepal, and Bhutan.

HINDU KUSH
KARAKORUM
PAKISTAN
CHINA
Mount Everest
HIMALAYAS
BHUTAN
NEPAL
River Ganges
INDIA
SRI LANKA

High heart of Asia
Along with the neighbouring Hindu Kush and Karakoram ranges, the Himalayas include all the world's mountains over 8,000 m (26,241 ft). Its snows feed the River Ganges in India.

THE HIGHEST MOUNTAINS ON EARTH

IMAGINE THE WORLD'S HIGHEST mountain. Perhaps you picture it towering tall above its neighbours. Or do you dream of a soaring, beautiful peak, circled by fluffy clouds? If this is how you imagine Everest, think again. Though it can be beautiful, other mountains are more spectacular. And despite its record-breaking height, from certain angles the peak actually looks lower than its neighbours. For Everest is the highest of a very, very high mountain range called the Himalayas. This range stretches 2,500 km (1,500 miles) across Asia, dividing India from China with a jagged, icy wall.

Everest's peak is 8,848 m (29,028 ft) above sea level.

South Ridge

NORTHEAST RIDGE
The Northeast Ridge is the route to the top from the Tibetan side of the mountain.

West Ridge

HIMALAYAS FROM SPACE
Seen from space, the snow-capped peaks of the Himalayas light up the heart of Asia. In this picture, the low plains of India are on the left, and the high plateau of the Chinese region of Tibet is on the right.

Plains of India

Snowy summits of Himalayan peaks

Tibetan plateau

MR EVEREST

Everest is named after Sir George Everest (1790–1866) who, as chief of the Survey of India, was in charge of the mapping of the subcontinent. But Sir George did not like the honour. In 1857, he objected that "Everest" could not be pronounced in local languages, or written in Hindi. Local people still call the mountain Chomolunga.

> "Sir, I have discovered the highest mountain in the world!"
>
> Radhanath Sikhdar, chief mathematician of the Survey of India speaking to the Surveyor General, 1852

Weather warning

Climbing in the Himalayas is made more difficult by the weather. In winter (November to March), cold winds are a hazard. The monsoon season, from May or June to September, brings heavy snows. Spring and autumn are therefore the best seasons for climbing.

VALLEY TOWN
Nepali people live in sheltered Himalayan valleys, in villages and small market towns.

SOUTH COL
The Southwest face, with the South Col at its highest point, seals the top of the Western Cwm.

LHOTSE
Everest's neighbour, Lhotse, is itself the fourth highest mountain in the world.

WESTERN CWM
This steep-sided valley is half filled by the glacier that carved it.

Khumbu glacier

A rock step under the Icefall breaks the glacier into huge chunks.

HIMALAYAN PEOPLE

The Tibetans who live on the northern Himalayan slopes are traditionally Buddhist nomads (wandering herders). By contrast, the Nepali people to the south are settled farmers, and mostly Hindus. The ancestors of the Sherpa people crossed the mountains bringing salt and wool from Tibet to barter (trade) for grain in Nepal.

Fanny tacked a "Votes for women" poster to her ice axe.

OUTLINE OF EVEREST

Shaped like a three-sided pyramid, Everest is hemmed in by glaciers. These rivers of ice have carved away the mountain, creating the three knife-edge ridges that separate the mountain's three faces. The summit is only 3,400 m (11,000 ft) above the foot of Everest, on the Khumbu Glacier. However, the glacier is itself nearly 5,500 m (18,000 ft) above sea level.

Suffragette pioneer

Women climbers have never been strangers to the Himalayas. In 1906, American traveller Fanny Workman (1859–1925) climbed 6,930 m (22,736 ft) to Pinnacle Peak. Fanny was a keen suffragette (campaigner for the right for women to vote) and she unveiled a poster at the top.

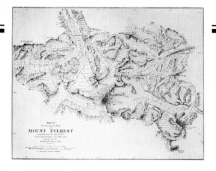

Mapping the mountain
To prepare for climbing the mountain, a British expedition took five surveyors to Everest in 1921. The information they collected helped to make the first accurate maps of the area. Using these, George Mallory, the leader, identified a route to the top via the North Col.

Andrew Irvine
George Mallory
Edward Norton
Noel Odell

The 1924 team
The leader of the 1924 expedition, General Bruce, caught malaria while hunting tigers on the way to Everest, and was replaced by Edward Norton. George Mallory, Norton's deputy, feared the mountain, and told a friend, "I don't expect to come back".

THE PIONEERS OF EVEREST

BRITISH GENTLEMEN IN CARDIGANS AND tweed jackets were the first Europeans to walk on Everest. A British team scouted the mountain in 1921. The following year they returned, and two men climbed to within 530 m (1,740 ft) of the summit. Encouraged by this feat, they mounted another expedition in 1924. Bad weather and altitude sickness twice drove the climbers back. But George Mallory, who had been on both these expeditions, was not discouraged. He was determined to have one last try and, on 8 June 1924, he set off for the summit with fellow climber Andrew Irvine. What happened that day remains one of the great mysteries of Everest.

The climb to Camp VI went well – all six climbers were in good form and the weather was fine.

Expedition leader, Edward Norton lay snowblind in a tent and did not see them leave.

7 June 1924 UP TO CAMP VI
Next day, Mallory, Irvine and four Sherpas pressed on to Camp VI. Mallory scribbled notes and the four Sherpas took them down to geologist Noel Odell, who was waiting at Camp V in case they needed help. The Sherpas left Mallory and Irvine fit and well, and with plenty of oxygen.

6 June 1924 LEAVING CAMP IV
The climbers were tackling the mountain from the north side. With eight Sherpas, Mallory and Irvine left Camp IV on the North Col to climb to camps that had already been established higher up the mountain.

Mallory   Irvine

*Dear Noel
We'll probably start early to-morrow (8th) in order to have clear weather. It won't be too early to start looking out for us either crossing the rockband under the pyramid or going up skyline at 8.0 p.m.
Yrs ever
G Mallory*

Mallory scribbled the note in pencil on a page torn from a pad.

Mallory's last note
In one of two last letters, Mallory said that he planned an early start. Yet the two climbers were very late reaching the step where Odell spotted them. Problems with oxygen may have delayed the pair.

> ❝ **"Because it's there."**
> George Mallory, 1923, when asked why he wanted to climb Everest ❞

Mallory had a "Vest-pocket" Kodak camera similar to this one.

Did they reach the summit?
Climbers still argue about whether Mallory and Irvine reached the summit. Perhaps the answer lies in Mallory's missing camera. Experts believe the icy climate may have preserved the film, which would contain pictures of the view from the top. Expeditions continue to search Everest for the camera.

MOVING DOTS
Later, Odell could not be sure whether he saw the two moving dots, either here below the second step, or below the first step.

Second step

MALLORY'S BODY
Mallory's body was found in this area in 1999. He was identified by a nametape on his jacket and letters in his pocket.

First step

Northeast ridge

The climbers were last seen as tiny dots making their way up a step of rock.

The rock step

A broken safety rope found on Mallory's body suggests that the climbers were tied together.

The climbers wore everyday clothing. If injured, they would have died of exposure very quickly.

> ❝ **"I noticed far away...a tiny object moving and approaching the rock step. A second object followed, and then...the scene became enveloped in cloud once more."**
> Noel Odell, 1924 ❞

8 June 1924

LAST SIGHTING
Mallory and Irvine planned to set off early for the summit. They still had a long way to go when Odell spotted them briefly at noon as he climbed to Camp VI. It was the last time Mallory and Irvine were seen alive.

WHAT HAPPENED?
Finding and rescuing the climbers was impossible, and their death remains a mystery. When Mallory's body was found in 1999, he had no oxygen, his leg was broken, and his snow goggles were in his pocket. This suggests that one or both climbers fell in the dark.

AN IMPOSSIBLE CHALLENGE?

IN 1933, TWO TINY AIRCRAFT BUZZED over the Himalayas towards Everest. The planes had special engines to climb in the thin air, and the crews wore electrically heated suits to avoid frostbite. Their mission was to swoop over Everest while filming and taking photographs of the mountain. Though the flight was eventually successful, it nearly ended in tragedy. A British climbing expedition that set off the same year failed, as did attempts in 1936 and 1938. When World War II broke out in Europe in 1939, the summit of Everest seemed as remote as ever.

First aerial view
This photograph of Everest's Northeast Face was taken by the first aerial reconnaissance (a survey carried out by aircraft) of Everest in 1933. The Everest Committee of the Royal Geographical Society, which organized British climbing expeditions to Everest, was able to use the aerial photographs to plan later assaults.

A plume of cloud, which looked like the smoke from a volcano, rose from Everest's peak.

As the aircraft approached the mountains, they were pulled down by a strong draught of air.

TAKE-OFF!
On 3 April 1933, two aircraft took off from a landing strip 240 km (150 miles) from Everest to take aerial photographs of the mountain. As they approached the summit, the pilots realized they were dangerously low and had to climb steeply to avoid crashing on the peak.

Unlike climbers, flyers cannot become acclimatized to altitude, and swiftly pass out without oxygen.

A CLOSE SHAVE
The flight nearly ended in disaster when the cameraman fell unconscious through lack of oxygen. Struggling to see what had happened, the pilot broke his own oxygen mask, and he had to fly home holding the mask in place with one hand.

GROUND WORK

In 1935, Eric Shipton led a small British expedition to Everest. His purpose was to train climbers and to survey the area for a later attempt. The team photographed the summit from many different viewpoints. Like all pre-World War II expeditions, they approached the mountain from the northern (Tibet) side.

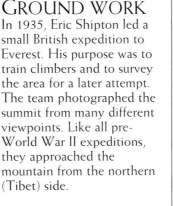

Oxygen improvements
Breathing apparatus improved with each expedition to Everest. The oxygen set made for the 1933 team (shown above) was less than half the weight of that used nine years before, but climbers still hated wearing it.

BEATEN BY SNOW

A small British expedition in 1938 was the last to attempt the mountain from the north. Bad weather defeated the climbers almost before they had started. The monsoon came early, blanketing Everest in deep snow. It was the last attempt on Everest before World War II.

ICEFALL APPROACH
Shipton's team climbed through the Icefall and nearly reached the Western Cwm.

The Yeti

ACCORDING TO NEPALI LEGEND, the Himalayan slopes are the home of a beast called the yeti, or "abominable snowman". In 1951, British climbers photographed what may have been yeti footprints.

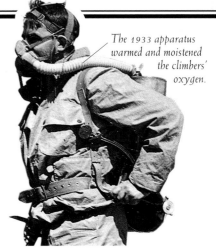

A terrifying beast?
Sherpas believe that there are two types of yeti and that only one attacks humans. Reports of attacks are very rare, and this illustration from 1960 is purely imaginary.

A NEW SOUTHERN ROUTE

In 1950, China invaded Tibet, closing northern routes to Everest. But the same year Nepal began to welcome foreigners, and an Anglo-American team trekked as far as the Khumbu Icefall. In 1951, Eric Shipton led a British team searching for possible routes to the top.

"The possibility of entering the unknown; the simple fact that it was the highest point on the world's surface – these things goaded us on... There was the challenge, and we would lay aside all else to take it up."

John Hunt, in his book
The Ascent of Everest, 1953

The British team planned to follow the route the Swiss had pioneered in 1952.

British army officer John Hunt, leader of the 1953 attempt on Everest

Warned by the Swiss of the hazards of the route, Hunt's team took ladders with them to cross the crevasses.

The Expedition of 1953

EXPLORING EVEREST'S LOWER SLOPES IN 1951 had made the British confident that they could reach the top the following year. To their dismay, the Nepali government allowed a Swiss expedition to try in 1952. The Swiss found a route to the South Col, but did not get to the summit. This left the way clear for a new British attempt at Everest in 1953.

Seven members of the British team cross a big crevasse above Camp III, April 1953.

> "The ascent of Everest was not the work of one day, nor even of those few unforgettable weeks in which we climbed... It is, in fact, a tale of sustained and tenacious endeavour by many, over a long period of time."
>
> John Hunt, from his book
> *The Ascent of Everest*, 1953

PLANNING TO BEAT THE MOUNTAIN

SO MUCH TO DO – AND SO LITTLE TIME! British expedition leader John Hunt had to choose a team, plan a route, buy and ship equipment – the list was endless. Hunt worked quickly. In a week he had devised a basic plan. Then he picked a team of climbers, several reserves, and a doctor. Four hectic months of meetings, testing, and training followed, and on 12 February the climbers boarded a ship bound for Bombay in India.

Royal Geographical Society
Organising the 1953 climb was the work of the Himalayan Committee of the British Royal Geographical Society (RGS). Since 1919, the RGS had controlled access to Everest by using its influence with the governments of Tibet, Nepal, and India.

THE TEAM
Hunt chose enough climbers so that three pairs could try for the summit, with others in reserve. The size of the team was limited by the weight of the equipment they would need.

John Hunt
The expedition leader John Hunt was an army officer with a "genius for organisation". He also had experience of climbing in both the Alps and the Himalayas.

FACT file

- All the equipment and food had been tested by Hunt and three other climbers in the Alps in midwinter.
- Hunt's wife and two friends sewed nametags into hundreds of garments to avoid arguments on the mountain.
- 12 porters were needed simply to carry the boxes of money to pay the wages of all the other porters.

Tom Bourdillon
Physicist Tom Bourdillon had been a member of the 1951 team that scouted routes up Everest.

Charles Evans
Surgeon Charles Evans was a very experienced climber. It was his fourth expedition to the Himalayas.

Edmund Hillary
New Zealand beekeeper Edmund Hillary had climbed the lower slopes of Everest in 1951.

Tenzing Norgay
Tenzing was a Sherpa *sirdar* (leader). He had climbed with the Swiss expedition of 1952 to 8,595 m (26,200 ft).

George Lowe
Teacher

Alfred Gregory
Travel agent

Mike Westmacott
Statistician

Wilfrid Noyce
Teacher and author

Charles Wylie
Army officer

Michael Ward
Doctor

George Band
Student

Griffith Pugh
Physiologist

Tom Stobbart
Cameraman

James Morris
Reporter

Six Sherpas went to the highest camps as part of the climbing party.

A team of nearly 30 Sherpas moved supplies and equipment the last stage of the journey to the high camps.

Around half the porters were women.

Around 450 porters were needed to carry loads of equipment, each weighing around 27 kg (60 lbs), through the foothills.

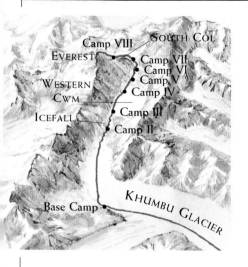

Route to the summit
Hunt planned to make two or three attempts at the summit, following the same route the Swiss had taken the previous year. But first the expedition had to ferry tonnes (tons) of equipment from their temporary base 24 km (15 miles) away, and set up a series of camps on the Khumbu Glacier in the Western Cwm.

EVEREST IN SIGHT

THE STRAGGLING LINE OF CLIMBERS and porters panted up the steep track. At the top they glimpsed a shining triangle of white snow in the far distance. Everest! It was still 80 km (50 miles) away, but this first view of the mountain was a magical moment. Some of the British climbers scrambled up trees for a better look. They didn't pause for long though – they had a long way to go. Although they had been walking for eight days, they were still only halfway to their first base camp at Thyangboche Buddhist monastery.

26 Mar 1953
THYANGBOCHE
The group took 17 days to walk from Kathmandu to Thyangboche. At a temporary base camp there, the Europeans got used to the high altitude, and tried out the oxygen apparatus on nearby peaks.

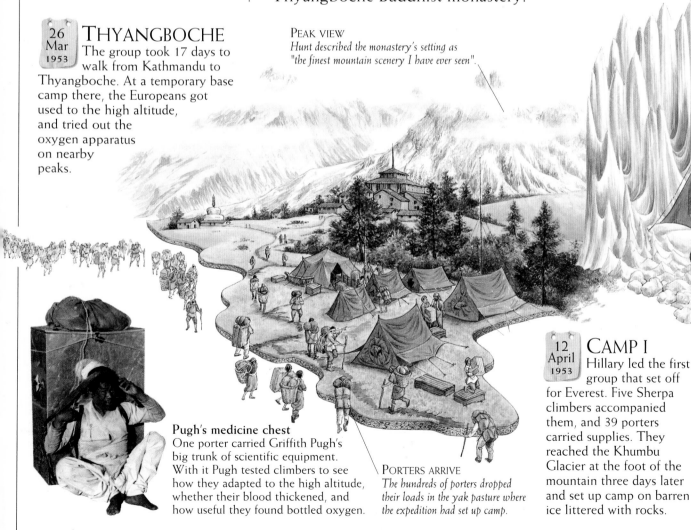

PEAK VIEW
Hunt described the monastery's setting as "the finest mountain scenery I have ever seen".

Pugh's medicine chest
One porter carried Griffith Pugh's big trunk of scientific equipment. With it Pugh tested climbers to see how they adapted to the high altitude, whether their blood thickened, and how useful they found bottled oxygen.

PORTERS ARRIVE
The hundreds of porters dropped their loads in the yak pasture where the expedition had set up camp.

12 April 1953
CAMP I
Hillary led the first group that set off for Everest. Five Sherpa climbers accompanied them, and 39 porters carried supplies. They reached the Khumbu Glacier at the foot of the mountain three days later and set up camp on barren ice littered with rocks.

Summit SOUTH SUMMIT SOUTH COL
Camp IX
Camp VIII
Camp VII
Camp VI
Camp V
Camp IV
ICEFALL
Camp III
Camp II
Base Camp

Route to the summit
By early May, most of the climbers were living at Camp IV, at 6,4501 m (21,200 ft). Hunt hoped that from a camp on the South Col, 1,400 m (4,600 ft) higher, it would be possible to reach the summit and return safely in one day. However, nobody had climbed that high before, and there might be unexpected problems on the South Ridge, or beyond the South Summit.

THE FINAL ASSAULT

"WILL I GO TO THE TOP?" THIS WAS the question on each climber's mind on the morning of 7 May. Expedition leader John Hunt had called a meeting. Everybody knew that he had chosen the climbers who would make the final assault on the summit, and that he would read out their names at the meeting. There had been plenty of time to choose. The climbers and Sherpas had been working together for nearly two months. Over the previous week, Hunt had watched the team on the glacier, moving up to a high base at Camp IV.

It was a difficult choice: there was only enough bottled oxygen for two pairs of climbers to attempt the

Hunt and Da Namgyal carried a tent and supplies to 8,300 m (27,350 ft) and then descended, completely exhausted.

TENT MEETING
The climbers met in the biggest tent, where they usually gathered for meals.

SLIPPERY SLOPES
A coating of snow made the steep slopes treacherous

NAMING THE TEAMS
7 May 1953
Hunt announced that Charles Evans and Tom Bourdillon would make the first attempt on the summit. Edmund Hillary and Tenzing Norgay were to be the second team. The other climbers would all have important jobs supporting these assaults.

THE FIRST ASSAULT
26 May 1953
Three weeks after the teams had been decided, Evans and Bourdillon set off from Camp VIII on the South Col. Hunt and five other climbers carried their supplies as far as they could, then watched enviously as the pair cut steps towards the summit. At first, Evans and Bourdillon climbed quickly, but by late morning mist and a snowfall were slowing them down.

summit. One team would use an "open circuit" oxygen system. This worked by enriching the air they breathed with oxygen from the bottles. The other pair would climb with a "closed circuit" system, which worked in the same way but also recycled the air they breathed out.

As the climbers crammed into the small dome tent, there was an excited atmosphere. John Hunt stood up to speak. Who had he chosen?

BREATHLESS
Evans and Bourdillon had problems with the closed-circuit oxygen apparatus.

DANGEROUS COULOIR
The slip in the couloir could have meant a fall of 300 m (1,000 ft).

Bourdillon rolled over and dug his axe into the ice.

DECISION TIME

By early afternoon, Evans and Bourdillon had reached the South Summit, just 90 m (300 ft) from the top of Everest. They were higher than anyone had climbed before, but they were running out of oxygen. They discussed whether it was safe to go on, and realized that they did not have enough oxygen or time to make it to the summit and back before it got dark. Disappointed, they turned back.

> " 'They're up! By God, they're up!' ...the clouds had cleared and he [Lowe] had seen the tiny figures of Evans and Bourdillon moving up on the South Summit...only 300 feet from the top."
>
> George Lowe, quoted by Edmund Hillary in *High Adventure*, 1955

AN EVENTFUL DESCENT

When the climbers reached the couloir (gully) down the South Col, they were very tired. Suddenly, Evans lost his footing and slid down the icy slope, pulling Bourdillon after him. Luckily, Bourdillon's quick thinking saved them. He stabbed his ice axe into the snow, and they slithered to a halt.

Exhausted return
Evans and Bourdillon staggered exhausted into Camp VIII late in the afternoon of the 26 May. They were coated with ice, and could hardly stand. After cups of soup, the two men told their story and described what they had learned about the route to the top.

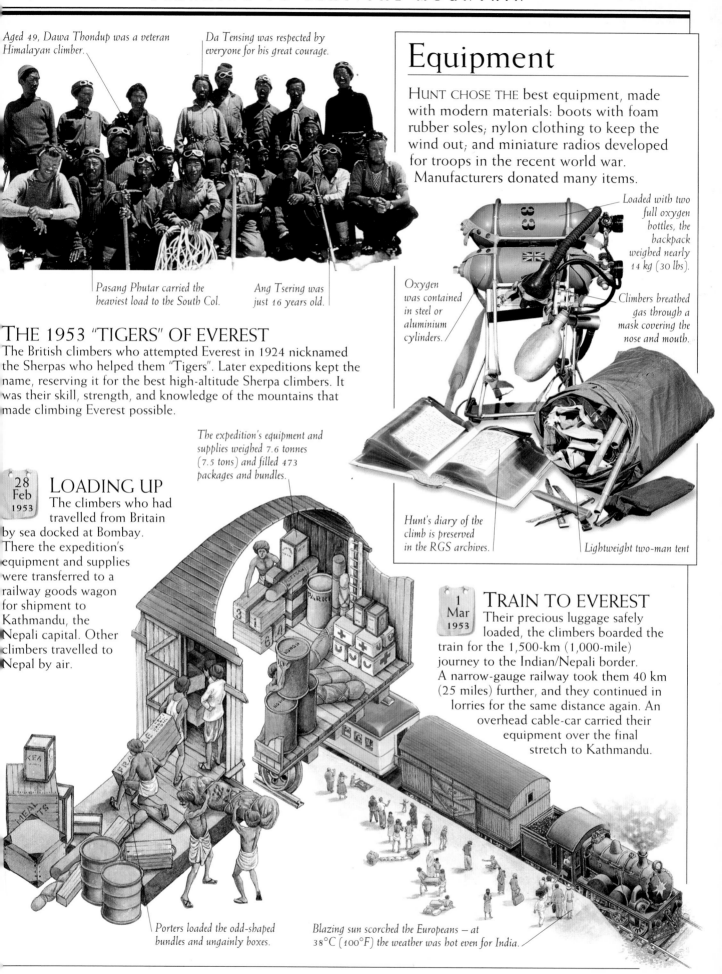

Aged 49, Dawa Thondup was a veteran Himalayan climber.

Da Tensing was respected by everyone for his great courage.

Pasang Phutar carried the heaviest load to the South Col.

Ang Tsering was just 16 years old.

Equipment

HUNT CHOSE THE best equipment, made with modern materials: boots with foam rubber soles; nylon clothing to keep the wind out; and miniature radios developed for troops in the recent world war. Manufacturers donated many items.

Loaded with two full oxygen bottles, the backpack weighed nearly 14 kg (30 lbs).

Oxygen was contained in steel or aluminium cylinders.

Climbers breathed gas through a mask covering the nose and mouth.

THE 1953 "TIGERS" OF EVEREST

The British climbers who attempted Everest in 1924 nicknamed the Sherpas who helped them "Tigers". Later expeditions kept the name, reserving it for the best high-altitude Sherpa climbers. It was their skill, strength, and knowledge of the mountains that made climbing Everest possible.

The expedition's equipment and supplies weighed 7.6 tonnes (7.5 tons) and filled 473 packages and bundles.

Hunt's diary of the climb is preserved in the RGS archives.

Lightweight two-man tent

28 Feb 1953 LOADING UP

The climbers who had travelled from Britain by sea docked at Bombay. There the expedition's equipment and supplies were transferred to a railway goods wagon for shipment to Kathmandu, the Nepali capital. Other climbers travelled to Nepal by air.

1 Mar 1953 TRAIN TO EVEREST

Their precious luggage safely loaded, the climbers boarded the train for the 1,500-km (1,000-mile) journey to the Indian/Nepali border. A narrow-gauge railway took them 40 km (25 miles) further, and they continued in lorries for the same distance again. An overhead cable-car carried their equipment over the final stretch to Kathmandu.

Porters loaded the odd-shaped bundles and ungainly boxes.

Blazing sun scorched the Europeans — at 38°C (100°F) the weather was hot even for India.

THE TRIUMPH!

"THE BRITISH ASSAULT ON EVEREST HAS failed," crackled the radio, "The expedition is withdrawing." The climbers awaiting Hillary and Tenzing's return chuckled. All-India Radio had got it wrong. Moments later, the climbers saw them and called out. Lowe, leading the group of descending climbers, waved ecstatically. They had done it! *The Times* newspaper reporter James Morris hurried to Base Camp. To ensure his paper would be first with the news, he typed in code. "Snow conditions bad" meant success. "Advanced base abandoned" stood for Hillary. Tenzing's code-name was "Awaiting improvement". Next morning, a runner took the message to the nearest radio transmitter so it could be sent to London.

International news
By 2 June the whole world knew that Hillary and Tenzing had climbed Everest. *The Times* of London was able to publish a unique colour supplement to celebrate the great achievement because their reporter James Morris was a member of the expedition.

> "Suddenly, the leading man in the party…raised his axe, pointing unmistakably towards the distant top of Everest; he made several vigorous thrusts. Far from failure, this was IT! They had made it!"
>
> John Hunt, expedition leader, from his book *The Ascent of Everest*, 1953

Lowe brought oxygen and a vacuum flask of hot soup up to Hillary and Tenzing.

THE MEETING
George Lowe climbed up from the South Col to meet the pair. He was the first to learn the news. "Well, George," Hillary told him,

CLIMBING DOWN
29 May 1953
The climb down from the summit was difficult and dangerous. Hillary and Tenzing were both exhausted. Snow had blown across many of the steps in the ice. Cutting new steps made them even more tired.

The ice of the Lhotse Glacier hid the group from view until they had almost reached Camp VII.

The second attempt

Evans and Bourdillon had not reached the summit but their attempt was a valuable lesson. It was now clear that Hillary and Tenzing could not get to the top directly from the South Col. They would have to start their dash to the summit from a new camp higher up on the South Ridge. So on 28 May, George Lowe, Alfred Gregory, and Ang Nyima set off to carry stores up the ridge. Hillary and Tenzing followed an hour or so later.

Sickness had put a Sherpa climber out of action, so the remaining climbers carried very heavy loads.

OXYGEN CRISIS
Flexing the wide rubber outlet tube forced out the ice that had blocked it.

The chips of ice, fell at dangerously high speed.

PITCHING CAMP

Hillary and Tenzing now had to put up their tent, but the only ledge they could find was very narrow. A fierce gale buffeted them as they struggled to put it up, but somehow they managed. After a meal of dates, sardines, and apricots, Hillary and Tenzing curled up in their sleeping bags. The wind, the cold, and the thin air meant neither slept much.

Oxygen bottles were used to anchor some of the guy ropes.

SHOWER OF ICE

28 May 1953

An advance party of three climbers led by Lowe, cut steps up to the South Ridge. As they climbed, they were showered with chips of ice cut away by the climbers above. Only when the danger had passed could they climb on and join the others. Together the five men reached 8,500 m (27,900 ft). Here the three support climbers left the supplies, and said goodbye to Hillary and Tenzing.

To save oxygen, the men had taken off their breathing apparatus, which made the job very tiring.

Both men slept wearing oxygen masks.

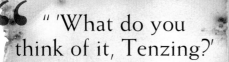

" 'What do you think of it, Tenzing?'

'Very bad, very dangerous.' "

Edmund Hillary and Tenzing Norgay, before they began their ascent of the South Summit, in Hillary's book, *High Adventure*, 1955

THE FINAL RIDGE
The last part of the ascent was along the ridge that lead to the summit. The rock step formed part of this ridge.

HUGS OF JOY
Forgetting their tiredness, the two climbers embraced each other.

TO THE TOP

The men's ordeal was not yet over. Above the rock step, the ridge continued to rise. Hillary cut steps in the snow, his energy fading. The climbing seemed endless. Finally, Hillary and Tenzing climbed a snowy dome, and looked around for the next ridge. They could go no further. It was 11:30 a.m., and they were standing on the summit of Everest.

ALMOST THERE...

29 May 1953

At 6:30 the following morning, the two men set off, and by 9 a.m. they had reached the South Summit. Then suddenly, Hillary noticed Tenzing gasping for air, and moving very slowly. Alarmed, he checked Tenzing's oxygen set and found it was completely blocked by ice. Fortunately Hillary shifted the blockage, and they climbed on.

Temperatures of -27°C (-32°F) froze Hillary's boots and he had to thaw them over the cooking stove in the morning.

When Hillary reached the top of the chimney the 12-m (40-ft) rope was taut – it had been only just long enough.

...THE FINAL STEP

The final obstacle was a sheer step of rock, and there was no way round it. However, ice clinging to one side had separated from the rock, leaving a fragile space between, called a chimney. Hillary made his way up the narrow gap, and then held the rope as Tenzing followed.

Celebration on the summit
Hillary took three pictures of Tenzing at the top, and the photograph above has since become a record of their incredible achievement. While Hillary took more photographs, Tenzing made a traditional Buddhist offering of sweet food (chocolate and biscuits) to the gods of the mountain.

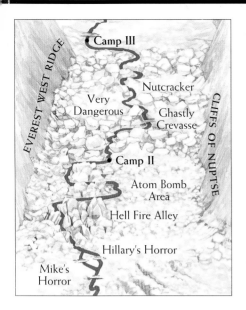

Camp III

EVEREST WEST RIDGE

Nutcracker

Very
Dangerous

Ghastly
Crevasse

CLIFFS OF NUPTSE

Camp II

Atom Bomb
Area

Hell Fire Alley

Hillary's Horror

Mike's
Horror

The track through the Icefall

The Icefall was the first major obstacle on the way to the summit. First, the climbers struggled through a maze of icy rubble. Higher up, they braved unstable blocks as big as houses and steeples of ice leaning at crazy angles. They nicknamed some obstacles after the climber who first tackled them.

HILLARY'S HORROR

The climbers had to take alarming risks in the Icefall. The first day, Hillary faced a crevasse 12 m (40 ft) wide. The only way to cross it was along a block of ice that was wedged in the top. The crossing was so terrifying that the crevasse was later named Hillary's Horror.

ICE CLIFF
Once on the far side, Hillary had to cut steps up a 7 m (20 ft) high ice wall.

ICE BRIDGE
With every step, Hillary was convinced he could feel the ice bridge quiver beneath him.

ROPED UP
Mike Westmacott gripped Hillary's safety rope.

STONY FOUNDATIONS
Building a base of stones lifted the tents clear of the glacier.

RST TENTS
e tiny base camp quickly panded when the other mbers arrived.

Warm and snug

Even down clothing uld not keep out the d, so when they had ssential work to do, e climbers retreated he warmest place – their sleeping bags.

SAFETY FIRST
Hillary's party protected the porters from the Icefall's worst dangers by using fixed ropes and ladders.

OVER THE ICEFALL

13 April 1953

In the Icefall the climbers had to walk beneath huge, unstable ice blocks and cross fragile snow bridges. After four days, Hillary's group had found a way through, and over the following week they made the route safe for porters so that supplies and equipment could be taken to Camp IV.

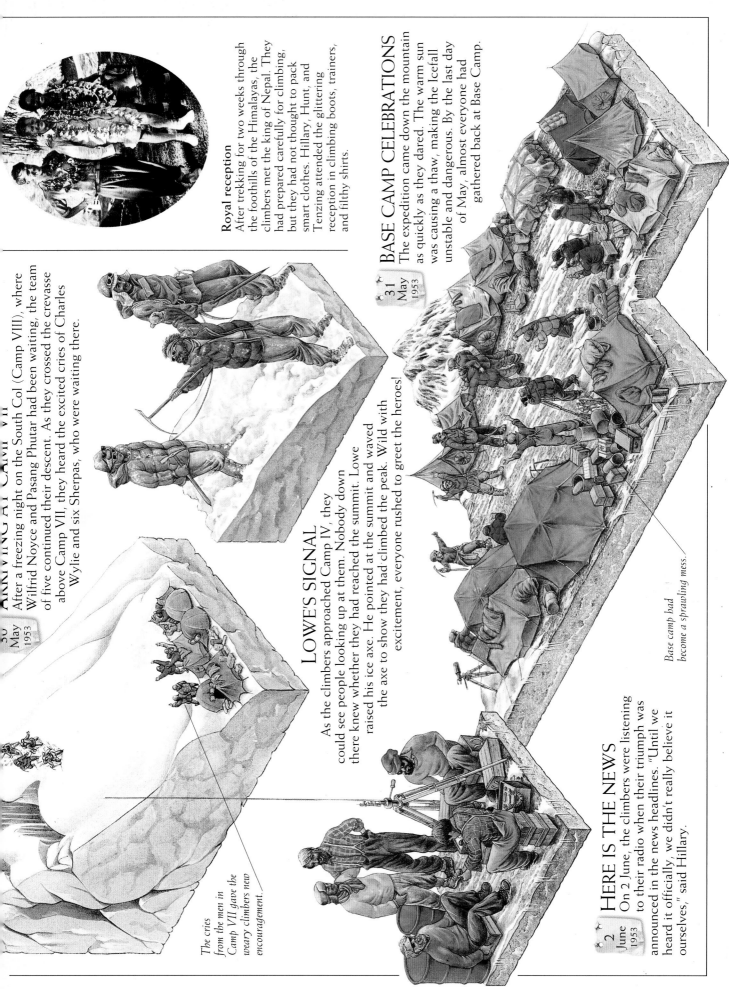

ARRIVING AT CAMP VII

After a freezing night on the South Col (Camp VIII), where Wilfrid Noyce and Pasang Phutar had been waiting, the team of five continued their descent. As they crossed the crevasse above Camp VII, they heard the excited cries of Charles Wylie and six Sherpas, who were waiting there.

The cries from the men in Camp VII gave the weary climbers new encouragement.

Royal reception

After trekking for two weeks through the foothills of the Himalayas, the climbers met the king of Nepal. They had prepared carefully for climbing, but they had not thought to pack smart clothes. Hillary, Hunt, and Tenzing attended the glittering reception in climbing boots, trainers, and filthy shirts.

LOWE'S SIGNAL

As the climbers approached Camp IV, they could see people looking up at them. Nobody down there knew whether they had reached the summit. Lowe raised his ice axe. He pointed at the summit and waved the axe to show they had climbed the peak. Wild with excitement, everyone rushed to greet the heroes!

BASE CAMP CELEBRATIONS

The expedition came down the mountain as quickly as they dared. The warm sun was causing a thaw, making the Icefall unstable and dangerous. By the last day of May, almost everyone had gathered back at Base Camp.

Base camp had become a sprawling mess.

HERE IS THE NEWS

On 2 June, the climbers were listening to their radio when their triumph was announced in the news headlines. "Until we heard it officially, we didn't really believe it ourselves," said Hillary.

33

In Hillary and Tenzing's footsteps

ENZING NORGAY HAD become a hero in Nepal. However, not every Sherpa praised him. "Now that you have done it," they told him, "nobody will want to climb Everest, and we will have no work." But they were wrong. Climbers kept on coming, seeking new and more exciting ways up. Behind them came tourists, eager to stand on the roof of the world, whatever the price.

> "Since Hillary and Tenzing reached the top, more than 1,050 people have stood on the world's highest summit. The busiest year was 1993, when 129 reached it and eight died."
>
> From *The Times* newspaper, London, UK, 4 May 1999

As lighter, better equipment made ascending Everest easier, climbers attempted new, seemingly impossible, routes.

Loose powder snow made steep slopes even more treacherous and caused dangerous avalanches.

British climber Dougal Haston on his way up Everest's dangerous Southwest Face in 1975.

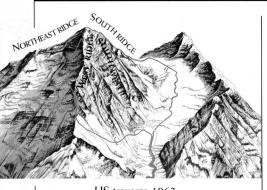

US traverse 1963
Great Britain 1975
Hillary and Tenzing 1953,
US 1963, Japan 1975, Sherpa 1991

Routes to the summit
The 1963 US expedition got two groups to the top by the South Ridge route, first climbed in 1953. Unsoeld and Hornbein also crossed Everest, going up the West Ridge and down the South Ridge. Bonington's 1975 expedition climbed the Southwest Face. The Sherpa and Japanese teams chose the South Ridge.

> **"In a dark and mysterious way, the deadly nature of the place has only strengthened Everest's grip on the world's imagination."**
>
> David F. Breashears, who has taken part in ten Everest expeditions, in *National Geographic*, September, 1997

DANGER AND DARING

HILLARY AND TENZING PROVED that climbing Everest was possible for a team with enough oxygen, supplies, and porters. Yet over the next ten years several huge and well-equipped expeditions failed. They discovered that without good luck and good weather Everest was a deadly place. However, Swiss and Chinese teams were successful, and in 1963 American climbers were the first to traverse Everest, taking one route up to the summit and another down.

OXYGEN TRAP
Bishop slipped on oxygen bottles the pair had thrown away.

LUCKY ESCAPE
Flames soon filled one end of the tent and the climbers struggled to get out.

GAS EXPLOSION
Jerstad was changing gas cylinders when the stove burst into flames. He and Bishop escaped injury, but their beards were singed and they were very shaken.

SUMMIT
3:30 p.m. When Jerstad and Bishop struggled up to the summit there was no sign of Willi Unsoeld and Tom Hornbein, who were crossing the mountain from the other side.

TIGHT GRIP
Jerstad grabbed Bishop, stopping his slide at 8,700 m (28,500 ft).

SCARY SLIP
11:15 a.m. The explosion delayed the pair by two hours, but they decided to press on. Then as they paused on a narrow ledge Bishop stumbled. Only quick thinking by his partner saved him from a deadly fall.

A BAD START
5:15 a.m. The 1963 American expedition made several ascents. A pair of climbers reached the top on 1 May. Then three weeks later, two more pairs planned to climb different routes and meet on the summit. Willi Unsoeld and Thomas Hornbein attempted a new route up the West Ridge. Lute Jerstad and Barry Bishop took the established southern route, but their assault began badly. In their camp high above the South Col, the cooking stove exploded.

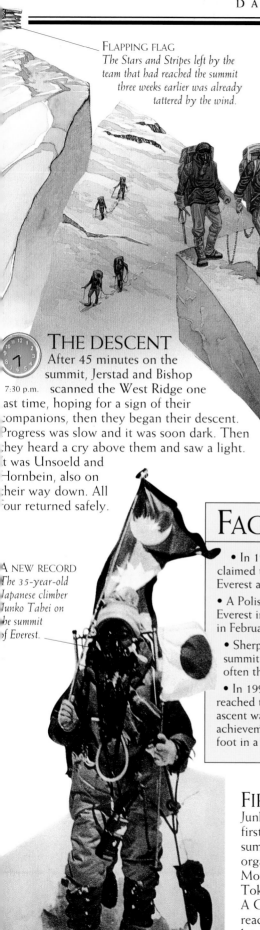

FLAPPING FLAG
The Stars and Stripes left by the team that had reached the summit three weeks earlier was already tattered by the wind.

STRANGE MEETING
In the darkness, Unsoeld and Hornbein could not be sure the two figures below them were their companions until Jerstad called out "Who are you?"

THE DESCENT

7:30 p.m.

After 45 minutes on the summit, Jerstad and Bishop scanned the West Ridge one last time, hoping for a sign of their companions, then they began their descent. Progress was slow and it was soon dark. Then they heard a cry above them and saw a light. It was Unsoeld and Hornbein, also on their way down. All four returned safely.

Jerstad and Bishop waited in the dark for the others to join them.

A NEW RECORD
The 35-year-old Japanese climber Junko Tabei on the summit of Everest.

NEW ROUTES

Many climbers looked for new routes to the top. A British expedition in 1975, led by Chris Bonington, chose the difficult Southwest Face. Four climbers, including Dougal Haston (above), reached the summit. Climber Mick Burke disappeared without trace.

Each Buddhist flag represents a prayer for success.

FACT file

• In 1960, three Chinese climbers claimed to have reached the summit of Everest at night.

• A Polish team was the first to climb Everest in winter, reaching the summit in February 1980.

• Sherpa Ang Rita has reached the summit of Everest ten times – more often than anyone else.

• In 1998, Welshman Tom Whittaker reached the summit of Everest. This ascent was a particularly remarkable achievement, because he had lost a foot in a car accident.

FIRST WOMEN

Junko Tabei became the first woman to reach the summit on an expedition organised by the Women's Mountaineering Club of Tokyo, Japan, in 1975. A Chinese group that reached the top 11 days later, also included a woman climber.

SHERPAS TO THE SUMMIT

Although they had played an important part in every earlier expedition, the first Sherpa-led team did not set off until 1991. Sonam Dendu, Ang Temba, and Apa Sherpa reached the summit. They were joined by American Pete Athans, one of a handful of foreign climbers supporting the team.

MODERN CLIMBING METHODS

COMPARED TO EVEREST'S EARLY HEROES, today's climbers have an easy time. Clever gadgets now secure climbers to fixed rope New materials have halved the weight of equipment, and clothes, boots, and sleeping bags are warmer. Yet these advances have not made climbing less challenging. Dedicated mountaineers have used the new technology and techniques to seek out ever more thrilling, dangerous, and extreme climbs.

CLIMBING BOOTS

Modern ice-climbing boots are similar to ski boots, and have an inner boot made of foam to protect against frostbite. They are less bulky than earlier boots, which were insulated with kapok (tree fibre), and they also have rigid soles. This is an important improvement. Climbers in the 1953 Everest expedition had boots that bent – as a result they snapped more than a dozen pairs of crampons (boot spikes).

TENT DESIGN

Traditional tents are designed for use on flat ground, which is rarely found on Everest! Newer designs have adjustable aluminium supports underneath them, that allow climbers to sleep on a level floor on the most uneven ledge.

A camp high in the Himalayas.

Learning safety

CLIMBING CAN BE DANGEROUS, and no one should ever attempt it alone. Anyone who wants to learn how to climb should contact a climbing club, where experienced climbers teach the basic skills in complete safety. They will also arrange supervised trips.

Climbing safely
Many mountaineering clubs have a climbing wall where beginners can learn to climb without risking injury.

An indoor climbing wall

FIXED BOLTS

Some climbers fix safety ropes to sheer cliffs by drilling bolts into the rock. However, traditional climbers disapprove of this, claiming that the bolts give an unsporting advantage.

Tying the strap to the wrist stops the climber losing this vital tool.

The jagged stainless-steel head grips ice and snow.

The handle is made of lightweight alloy or carbon fibre, and has a rubber grip.

ICE AND SNOW

New materials have made the modern ice axe safer and lighter. The shape of the axe has changed, too. A curved shaft and adjustable head make it easier to swing when cutting steps, yet it also grips snow well enough to stop a fall.

Using ropes and other devices has made exciting new climbs possible.

ROPES AND GADGETS

The use of ropes has changed dramatically since 1953, when climbers relied on ropes only in emergencies. Now climbers on difficult rock faces expect to use ropes to break their fall. Karabiners – the traditional ring clips climbers use with ropes – are now lighter and stronger, and there are new safety devices, such as the jumar. This is a clamp that moves up a safety rope but not down.

Jumar

Karabiner

Safety ropes are attached to a harness around a climber's waist and legs.

Rock protection

CLIMBERS TODAY use safety anchors, called nuts. They fit them into cracks in the rock. By clipping a rope onto the nut, climbers limit how far they can fall.

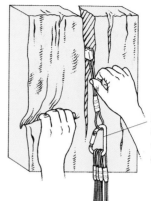

Nuts come in many sizes to fit all cracks.

Nuts are often kept on a karabiner, to reduce the chances of dropping them.

1 The leading climber chooses a nut that fits neatly into the crack. The shape of the rock must hold the nut fast.

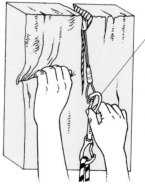

This arrangement of two karabiners is called a quickdraw. It reduces the friction of the rope on the nut, which could cause it to pop out!

2 Clipping a karabiner through the "tail" of the nut allows the climber to fix the safety rope to it. He or she can now climb higher in safety.

The nut is wriggled free and pulled out, but a tightly-jammed nut may need a special tool to get it out.

3 The final climber can safely remove the nut – it is no longer needed because the leader will have secured the rope higher up the rock face.

DESTINATION EVEREST

AFTER HILLARY AND TENZING'S EPIC CLIMB, Everest came to represent the ultimate human challenge – and climbers rushed to try it. Trekkers came too – just to look. Many of these outsiders cared little for Nepali traditions, and they harmed the fragile Himalayan environment. The mountain itself became a rubbish tip. Today, things have improved. Tough new laws for tourists are slowly reducing the damage, and aid schemes are improving life for the people who live in Everest's shadow.

TREKKERS' FUEL

Until recently, countless trees were felled to fuel the campfire of Western trekkers. As a result deforestation became a serious problem. Today, visitors must bring fuel with them.

JOIN THE QUEUE
In May 1996, impatient climbers had to queue for their moment of glory "at the top of the world".

PARADISE LOST

The picture above shows the sad state of Camp I in 1996. Even in 1953 rubbish was a problem, and conditions soon got worse when other expeditions camped there. The mess is not only unsightly – the dirt also causes health problems. The site improved when Nepal's Ministry of Tourism began to fine climbers who left anything behind, and now even rubbish and sewage are removed.

Everest's victims

CLIMBERS DIE ON EVEREST MOST years because, in their zeal to reach the top, they ignore the mountain's dangers. The frozen corpses of failed climbers litter the slopes and act as grisly reminders of the risks.

Tragic self-portrait
Climber Bruce Herrod photographed himself at the top of Everest after a solo ascent in May 1996. Sadly, he died on his way down. His body and camera, which contained this picture, were found the following year.

CROWDED MOUNTAIN

Since 1953, more than a thousand people have reached the summit of Everest. This may not seem like many, but the climbing season is short, so everyone is trying to reach the top at the same time – most of them by the same route. At the busiest times, there simply isn't space for everyone to stand on the summit.

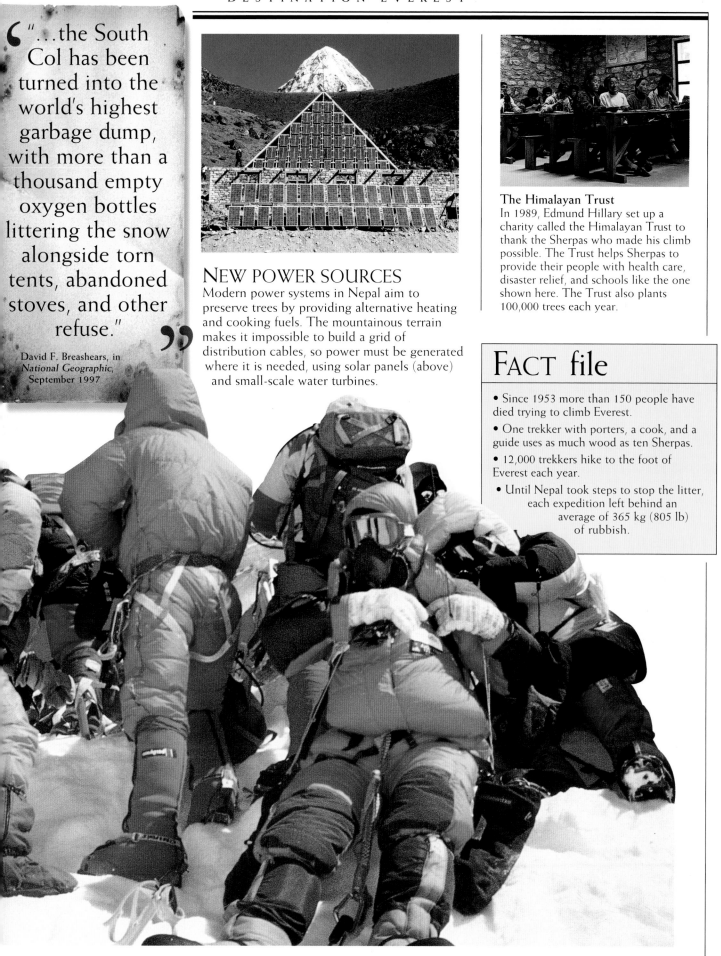

❝ "...the South Col has been turned into the world's highest garbage dump, with more than a thousand empty oxygen bottles littering the snow alongside torn tents, abandoned stoves, and other refuse." ❞

David F. Breashears, in *National Geographic*, September 1997

NEW POWER SOURCES

Modern power systems in Nepal aim to preserve trees by providing alternative heating and cooking fuels. The mountainous terrain makes it impossible to build a grid of distribution cables, so power must be generated where it is needed, using solar panels (above) and small-scale water turbines.

The Himalayan Trust
In 1989, Edmund Hillary set up a charity called the Himalayan Trust to thank the Sherpas who made his climb possible. The Trust helps Sherpas to provide their people with health care, disaster relief, and schools like the one shown here. The Trust also plants 100,000 trees each year.

FACT file

- Since 1953 more than 150 people have died trying to climb Everest.
- One trekker with porters, a cook, and a guide uses as much wood as ten Sherpas.
- 12,000 trekkers hike to the foot of Everest each year.
- Until Nepal took steps to stop the litter, each expedition left behind an average of 365 kg (805 lb) of rubbish.

Alpine pioneers in the Himalayas
Messner and Habeler were not the first to reject the "big expedition". In 1895, Alfred Mummery tackled peaks with just two companions, and before 1921, Alexander Kellas (above) had climbed in the Himalayas with local porters.

Everest without oxygen
Italian Reinhold Messner (left) and Austrian Peter Habeler (right) made history in 1978 when they scaled Everest without oxygen. Messner is perhaps the greatest Himalayan mountaineer of all time, and was the first to climb all the mountains in the world over 8,000 m (26,241 ft).

A NEW WAY OF CLIMBING

OVER THE YEARS, METHODS OF CLIMBING Everest changed. Ropes fixed to the mountain made it seem safe, and this once impossible peak was becoming a tourist trek. Some climbers looked for new thrills, such as returning to the roots of mountaineering – when climbers in the Alps had reached summit in pairs or small groups using basic equipment. In 1975, Reinhold Messner and Peter Habeler reached the 8,068-m (26,470-ft) summit of Hidden Pea in the Himalayas, using this "alpine style" of climbing. They showed that Himalayan climbers did not need oxygen and hundreds of porters. Suddenly there was a daring new challenge: was it possible to climb Everest alpine style, or even alone? Messner decided to find out.

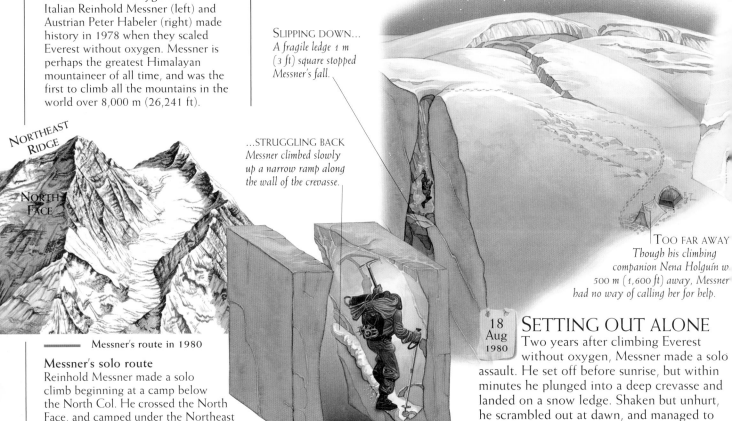

SLIPPING DOWN...
A fragile ledge 1 m (3 ft) square stopped Messner's fall.

...STRUGGLING BACK
Messner climbed slowly up a narrow ramp along the wall of the crevasse.

TOO FAR AWAY
Though his climbing companion Nena Holguín w 500 m (1,600 ft) away, Messner had no way of calling her for help.

NORTHEAST RIDGE

NORTH FACE

——— Messner's route in 1980

Messner's solo route
Reinhold Messner made a solo climb beginning at a camp below the North Col. He crossed the North Face, and camped under the Northeast Ridge. From there he dashed to the summit.

18 Aug 1980 SETTING OUT ALONE

Two years after climbing Everest without oxygen, Messner made a solo assault. He set off before sunrise, but within minutes he plunged into a deep crevasse and landed on a snow ledge. Shaken but unhurt, he scrambled out at dawn, and managed to climb to 7,800 m (25,590 ft).

Essential equipment

MESSNER CARRIED almost nothing to the top of Everest, but his solo climb is an extreme example of alpine style. Most alpine climbers carry a little more equipment, especially if the mountain is technically difficult.

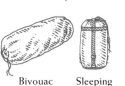

The rucksack holds everything.

Bivouac tent

Sleeping bag

Foam mattress

Stove

Ice axe

Crampons

Mitts

Goggles

Food

Camera

Rock-climbing equipment

Equipment for snow and ice

A tripod left by climbers in 1975 marked the top.

Screwed to his ice axe, Messner's camera recorded proof of his triumph.

TO THE TOP

20 Aug 1980
The next morning, taking only his ice axe and camera, Messner set off for the summit. Tormented by the thin air, he reached the top at 3:20 p.m. He hardly had the energy to take a picture of himself. The summit was covered in thick cloud, just as it had been in 1978, and he couldn't see anything.

BACK TO NENA

21 Aug 1980
After a sleepless night, Messner set off down the mountain. In the tent he left everything except his camera, extra gloves, and sunglasses. Suffering from exhaustion, dehydration, and heat stroke, he wept with relief when his friend Nena greeted him.

HIGH CAMP
Messner wanted to photograph himself by the tent, but he was too tired to set up the camera.

FIGHTING EXHAUSTION

19 Aug 1980
On the second day, Messner dumped food and cooking gas to save weight. Deep snow, then fog meant he made slow progress. When he finally pitched his tiny tent on a snow-covered rock ledge he was exhausted. This, together with the lack of oxygen, caused him to hallucinate, and he imagined a companion who urged him to melt snow for a life-saving drink.

Stage by stage

NOT ALL CLIMBS are possible in pure alpine style. Another technique, known as capsule climbing, divides a mountain into stages. Climbers fix ropes, but as they complete a stage, they remove them and use them for the next section.

Capsule climbing in the Himalayas

How MOUNTAINS FORM

THE EARTH'S CRUST (outer shell) is split into vast, rocky plates that move very slowly. Where two plates meet they either move apart, slide past each other, or one slips underneath the other. Mountain ranges form when the rocky plates collide. They buckle or crack pushing the Earth's crust upwards.

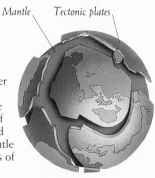

Tectonic plates
The Earth's crust is broken up into eight large and several smaller pieces known as "tectonic plates". These float on a thick layer of half-melted rock, called the mantle. As the mantle slowly flows, the plates of the crust move.

Mantle *Tectonic plates*

CRUCIAL COLLISION
About 180 million years ago, the tectonic plate on which India now lies began to move slowly northwards towards the Eurasian plate. Their collision forced rock upwards to form the Himalayas.

Indo-Australian plate *As the plates moved closer the ocean between them narrowed.* *Mountains formed here* *Eurasian plate* *Molten rock also pushed up the crust.*

Seventy million years ago
As the plates moved together, the Indo-Australian plate slid beneath the Eurasian plate. Rock was pushed upwards and mountains formed where the plates met.

The plate carrying India was dragged under the Eurasian plate. In the heat of the mantle, the plate started to melt.

Rivers carried soil into the ocean. *This is now Tibet* *Mountain rock began to be eroded by the weather.*

Fifty million years ago
The Indo-Australian plate plunged under the Eurasian plate and forced up the flat region now called Tibet. As rain eroded the newly-formed mountains, soil filled in the ancient ocean. The sunken crust melted into the mantle creating molten rock that rose upwards.

The ocean filled up with soil.

An aerial view
From a spacecraft, the snow-covered peaks of the Himalayas make scarcely a bump in the Earth's curving shape.

The plate containing India continues to push northwards, buckling the Eurasian plate.

Sediments are raised and folded to create the Himalayas.

INDIA

SRI LANKA

River Ganges

HIMALAYAS

As clouds rise over the Himalayas they deposit rain on the Indian side of the mountains but leave much of Tibet a desert.

TIBET

Continental crust is above sea level.

Formation of the Himalayas
Compared to other mountain ranges, the Himalayas formed very recently – just 600,000 years ago, when dinosaurs stalked the Earth. It was around this time that the upwards movement of molten rock in the mantle, pushed up the crust above it. The combination of the impact of the rocky plates and the pressure of the rising molten rock, made the Himalayas into the highest mountain range in the world.

Oceanic crust is below sea level.

• Mount Everest

Glaciers (moving ice rivers) have cut the steep sides of the mountains.

World's highest mountain
The rock of Mount Everest formed from mud pushed up from the ancient ocean floor when the Indo-Australian plate slid under the Eurasian plate. As a result, sea-bed fossils can be found on the world's highest mountain.

Types of mountain

THE HIMALAYAS ARE FOLD MOUNTAINS, formed by the creasing of the Earth's crust. Besides fold mountains, there are three other types of mountain, each named after the way they were formed.

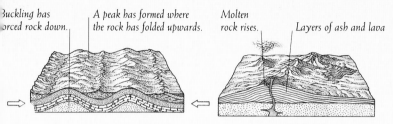

Buckling has forced rock down.

A peak has formed where the rock has folded upwards.

Molten rock rises.

Layers of ash and lava

Fold mountain
Sideways pressure makes the Earth's crust crumple into fold mountains. All the world's highest mountain ranges are formed this way.

Volcanic mountain
Hot rock bursting up through the Earth's crust can form a volcanic mountain. Lava and ash usually build up to form cone-shaped mountains.

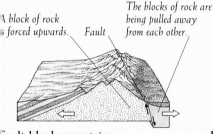

A block of rock is forced upwards.

Fault

The blocks of rock are being pulled away from each other.

Fault

Central block of rock has risen.

Fault

Fault-block mountains
Where the Earth's crust cracks, along lines called faults, movement in the crust can lift blocks of rock high above the surrounding land.

Dome mountain
When a large chunk of the Earth's surface is lifted without breaking, a dome mountain forms. It usually has a flat or dome-shaped top.

Mountain terms

CLIMBERS HAVE THEIR own special terms for different parts of mountains. Below are explanations of the words used by climbers to describe the main features of Everest.

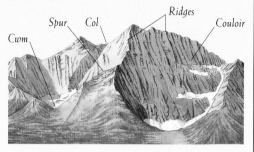

Cwm *Spur* *Col* *Ridges* *Couloir*

Col
The lowest point in a ridge, often between two summits.

Couloir
A steeply-sloping gully or gorge that cuts into the side of a mountain.

Cwm
A bowl-shaped valley on a hillside, cut out by the back of a glacier.

CHIMNEY

Chimney
A vertical crack in rock or ice that is wide enough to climb up.

Ridge
A high, narrow line of rock formed where two rock faces meet.

Spur
A small ridge that juts out from a main ridge or from another part of the mountain.

GLACIERS

Snow that falls high up on a mountain never melts. Instead it turns to ice, which collects in hollows and then slides slowly downhill as a glacier – a river of ice. Three glaciers created Everest, and smoothed the valleys around it into deep U shapes.

The sides of a glaciated valley are steep.

The glacier slides downhill a metre (yard) a day or less.

The glacier melts to form a lake.

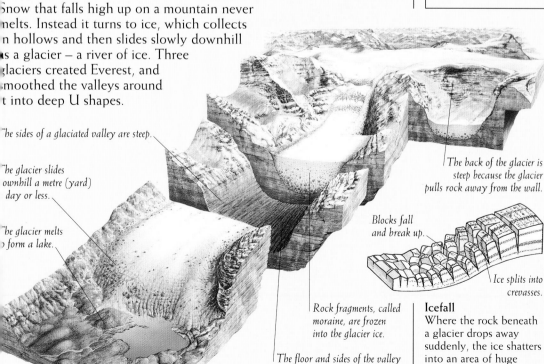

The back of the glacier is steep because the glacier pulls rock away from the wall.

Blocks fall and break up.

Ice splits into crevasses.

Rock fragments, called moraine, are frozen into the glacier ice.

Icefall
Where the rock beneath a glacier drops away suddenly, the ice shatters into an area of huge blocks, called an icefall.

The floor and sides of the valley are gouged out by the rocky ice.

Shaping Everest
The pyramid shape of Everest is clear in the centre of this picture taken from space. It is also easy to make out the three glaciers that have shaped the mountain: the Khumbu glacier, the Rongbuk glacier, and the Kangshung glacier.

MOUNTAINS OF THE WORLD

Mt. McKinley, Alaska, USA, North America 6,194 m (20,320 ft)

Mt. Everest, Nepal/China, Asia, 8,848 m (29,028 ft)

Aconcagua, Argentina, South America, 6,960 m (22,843 ft)

El'brus, Russia, Europe, 5,642 m (18,510 ft)

Kilimanjaro, Tanzania, Africa, 5,895 m (19,340 ft)

Mt. Wilhelm, Papua New Guinea, Australasia, 4,884 m (16,024 ft)

Vinson Massif, Antarctica, 5,140 m (16,863 ft)

FORCES DEEP IN THE EARTH'S crust have pushed up mountains on every continent. However, mountain-building forces do not push evenly. In North America the Rocky Mountains tower over the west of the continent, while to the east there's hardly a hill for 1,500 km (1,000 miles). Height varies dramatically, too. The highest peak in Australia is under 5,000 m (1,600 feet), which is lower than a foothill in the Himalayas.

THE WORLD'S MOUNTAIN RANGES

The longest range of mountains on Earth stretches for 30,900 km (19,200 miles) under the Pacific Ocean. Above sea level, the longest range is the Andes in South America, at 7,200 km (4,475 miles).

Great peaks

One of the great climbing challenges, known as the "Seven Summits", is to reach the summit of the highest peak in each continent. The first person to achieve this was American Dick Bass, when he climbed Everest in 1985. It is difficult to measure the height of a mountain exactly, and surveys often give different results. The Himalayas, which are still being formed, are rising 6 cm (over 2 in) a year. Recent satellite surveys have measured Everest at 8,863 m (29,078 ft).

COMPARATIVE SIZE OF THE HIGHEST PEAK ON EACH CONTINENT

Mt. Everest, 8,848 m (29,028 ft)

Kanchenjunga, 8,598 m (28,208 ft)

Makalu, 8,480 m (27,821 ft)

Nanga Parbat, 8,126 m (26,660 ft)

Dhaulagiri, 8,172 m (26,811 ft)

The mighty Himalayas

In the illustration above showing the Himalayas, five of the dozen peaks higher than 8,000 m (26,248 ft) are shown. Nine of the world's 10 highest mountains are in the Himalayas. The second highest peak in the world, called K2, lies in the Karakoram range just to the east of the Himalayas. K2 measures 8,611 m (28,250 ft).

The Alaska Range includes the continent's highest mountain, Mt. McKinley.

The Pyrenees separate France from Spain.

The Alps are the highest area in Europe.

The Caucasus mountains mark the boundary of Europe and Asia.

The Karakoram are the world's second-highest range.

The Himalayas dominate the centre of Asia.

The Rockies are North America's mountainous spine.

The Mid-Atlantic Ridge is an undersea range that rises 4,000 m (13,120 ft) from the ocean floor.

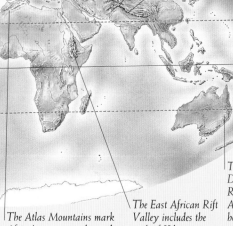

Mountain facts

- The Earth is not a perfect sphere. It bulges around the middle. This means that the peak farthest from the Earth's core is not Everest but Chimborazo in the Andes. It is 2,150 m (7,052 ft) higher than Everest.
- Mauna Kea in Hawaii rises 10,205 m (33,472 ft) from the floor of the Pacific Ocean, but only 4,205 m (13,792 ft) are above sea level.
- Climbers weigh less on top of tall mountains. They are farther from the centre of the Earth, where the pull of gravity is stronger. The difference is too small to make climbing easier.

The Andes tower over South America's west coast.

The Atlas Mountains mark Africa's snowy northern edge.

The East African Rift Valley includes the peak of Kilimanjaro.

The Great Dividing Range separates Australia's dry heart from the green coast.

EVEREST TIMELINE

FOR OVER A CENTURY, EVEREST has been the ultimate challenge for climbers. The number of Everest expeditions increased greatly in the 1970s. The list below highlights the most important milestones.

Pressure from India's British rulers kept other nations off Everest until India's independence in 1947.

1852
Survey of India
British surveyors in India identified Everest as the world's highest mountain.

1883
Himalayan climbing
Briton W. W. Graham was the first to climb in the Himalayas for sport.

EARLY ICE
AXE AND
COVER

1885
The Everest challenge
It was first proposed that it might be possible to climb Everest.

1919
Noel explores
Disguised as an Indian, British army officer John Noel explored Sikkim and Tibet and got closer to Everest than any European before him.

1921
British take a look
George Mallory led a British team exploring Everest from the north.

SNOW GOGGLES

1922
Climbing with oxygen
British climbers returned to Everest and climbed over 8,000 m (26,248 ft) using oxygen. An avalanche killed seven of the Sherpas in the party.

1924
Mallory and Irvine
Climbing higher than ever before, these two Britons lost their lives in a bid to reach the top.

1934
Lone climber dies
After travelling to Everest in secret, Briton Maurice Wilson died trying to reach the summit alone. Later, a Canadian (1947) and a Dane (1951) made similar attempts, but these also failed.

A HIGH CAMP

USING A
SAFETY
ROPE

1935–6
British try again
Another survey of the mountain was completed in 1935. British climbers returned the following year, but were defeated by the bad weather.

1950
Southern route opens
Tibet closed its borders, forcing climbers to approach Everest from a newly opened southern route through Nepal.

1951
British explorers
A British reconnaissance expedition successfully pioneered a route up the Khumbu Glacier.

1952
Swiss near-miss
In two expeditions, Swiss climbers reached the South Col.

1953
Success at last!
New Zealander Edmund Hillary and Sherpa Tenzing Norgay reached Everest's summit in a British-led expedition.

1956
Double triumph
A Swiss expedition climbed both Everest and Lhotse – the world's fourth highest peak.

1960
Chinese summit
Three Chinese climbers reached the top at night.

1963
First traverse
US climbers were the first to cross Everest via the summit.

1965
India's third try
After two earlier Indian expeditions had ended in failure, a third attempt got nine Indian climbers to the top.

1973
Italian expedition
Eight Italian climbers reached the summit by the South Col route.

1975
First women summit
In separate Chinese and Japanese attempts, two women reached the top.

1976
Preserving Everest
Sagarmatha National Park was established to protect the Everest region from damage by climbers, tourism, and development.

1977
South Korean success
Two climbers from a South Korean expedition reached the summit.

THE DESCENT

1978
Alpine style
Italian Reinhold Messner and Austrian Peter Habeler showed it was possible to climb Everest without oxygen.

1980
Alone at the top
Reinhold Messner became the first to reach the summit alone.

1980
Winter ascent
Two Poles were the first to climb Everest during the winter months.

1980
Spanish success
A 1974 Spanish attempt had ended in failure, but in 1980 a Basque team reached the summit.

1982
Canadians climb
Despite losing four climbers in accidents in the Icefall, a large Canadian team got six members to the top.

1984
Clean up
Thirty-six climbers from the Nepalese police force cleared some of the rubbish and bodies from the mountain.

1985
Norwegian record
An expedition from Norway got 17 people to the top. Dick Bass, a 55-year-old American was the oldest climber to have reached the summit.

1991
Sherpas summit
A Sherpa-only group reached the summit.

1993
Spring cleaning
A two-year clean-up was begun by the Nepal Mountaineering Association.

1996
Storm tragedy
The deaths of nine climbers led guides to insist that everyone who joined expeditions should have at least some climbing experience.

1996
Ten times up
Sherpa Ang Rita broke records when he got to the summit for the tenth time without oxygen.

CHAMOIX

1999
Mallory found
A US team trying to solve the riddle of Mallory and Irvine's disappearance found and buried the body of George Mallory.

Index

Acknowledgments

The publisher would like to thank:
Alex Messenger at the British
Mountaineering Council, Mark
Brewster, Len Reilly, David Torr,
and Walt Unsworth for specialist
information; Robert Graham for
research; Sheila Collins and Polly
Appleton for design assistance;
Carey Scott for editorial help; Frank
Bennet of Lyon Equipment and Paul
Simpkiss of DMM International Ltd.
for pictures of climbing equipment;
Chris Bernstein for the index.

The publisher would like to thank
the following for their kind

permission the reproduce their
photographs:

t=top, b=below, l=left, r=right,
c=centre

Alpine Club Library: 42tl; Aurora &
Quanta Productions Inc.: Robb
Kendrick 37br; Chris Bonington
Picture Library: 38br, 39bl; Doug
Scott 34–35, 37tr, 39tl; Leo
Dickinson 42cl; John Barry 43br;
Bridgeman Art Library, London/
New York: Christie's Images,
London, UK 6–7; Fitzwilliam
Museum, University of Cambridge,

UK 8br; Giraudon 14–15; British
Mountaineering Council: 38bl.
Corbis UK Ltd: Jon Sparks 38tl;
David Samuel Robbins 40tr; Alison
Wright 41ct; DK Picture Library:
19tr; DMM International: 39cl;
Mary Evans Picture Library: 9br,
17br, 20tl, 21br; John Frost
Historical Newspapers: The Sunday
Times 32tl; Hulton Getty: 9tr; Lyon
Equipment: 39tr, 39cr; Mountain
Camera/John Cleare: 37bl;
N.A.S.A.: 16bl, 45br; John Noel
Photographic Collection: 18cl, 19tl.
Popperfoto: Reuters 8bl; Royal
Geographical Society Picture

Library: 9cr, 13tl, 13c, 17tl, 17tr,
17cr, 17tl, 18tl, 21tl, 21tr, 21cl, 21c, 22tr,
22–23, 24cl, 25tr, 26bl, 27bl, 29b,
31br, 33tl, 41tr; Alfred Gregory 2c,
13tr, 25tl; Bruce Herrod 40c, 40bl;
Science Photo Library: Geospace
44tr; Woodfin Camp & Associates:
Neil Beidleman 40–41.

Jacket:
Chris Bonington Picture Library:
front br; Mountain Camera/John
Cleare: front inside flap; John
Noel Photographic Collection:
back br; Royal Geographical
Society: back cr.